Disability PRIDE

Listening Matters

Jill Keppeler

PowerKiDS press

Published in 2026 by The Rosen Publishing Group, Inc.
2544 Clinton Street, Buffalo, NY 14224

First Edition

Editor: Danielle Haynes
Book Design: Leslie Taylor

Photo Credits: Cover Dragana Gordic/Shutterstock.com; (series background) P.siripak/Shutterstock.com; (series disability pride colors) rudall30/Shutterstock.com; p. 5 Ground Picture/Shutterstock.com, (flag sidebar) Maxim Studio/Shutterstock.com; p. 7 Belish/iStockphoto.com; p. 9 paulaphoto/Shutterstock.com; p. 11 Lopolo/Shutterstock.com; pp. 13, 17 wavebreakmedia/Shutterstock.com; p. 15 India Picture/Shutterstock.com; p. 19 MAYA LAB/Shutterstock.com; p. 21 SeventyFour/Shutterstock.com.

Cataloging-in-Publication Data

Names: Keppeler, Jill.
Title: Listening matters / Jill Keppeler.
Description: Buffalo, New York : PowerKids Press, 2026. | Series: Disability pride | Includes glossary and index.
Identifiers: ISBN 9781499457032 (pbk.) | ISBN 9781499457049 (library bound) | ISBN 9781499457056 (ebook)
Subjects: LCSH: Listening–Juvenile literature. | Interpersonal communication–Juvenile literature. | People with disabilities–Juvenile literature. | Disabilities–Juvenile literature.
Classification: LCC BF323.L5 K47 2026 | DDC 153.68–dc23

Manufactured in the United States of America

Some of the images in this book illustrate individuals who are models. The depictions do not imply actual situations or events.

CPSIA Compliance Information: Batch #CWPK26. For Further Information contact Rosen Publishing at 1-800-237-9932.

Contents

Communication Is Key

Everyone on this planet is different. We're different shapes and shades. We like different things, and we learn in different ways. This is one of the reasons why it's so important to communicate with each other! To communicate means to use words, sounds, signs, or behaviors to show your ideas, thoughts, and feelings.

But just as it's important to communicate, it's also important to listen or pay attention when other people communicate with you. Because we're all different, we can all want different things. To be a good **ally** to people with disabilities—even if you also have a disability—you need to listen!

The disability pride flag was created to show acceptance and respect for people who have disabilities. Each color is for a different type of disability.

- The gray background is in honor of those who've died.
- Green is for disabilities that have to do with the senses.
- Blue is for those that have to with the mind and emotions.
- White stands for unseen disabilities, as well as those that haven't been diagnosed, or found out.
- Gold is for **neurodiversity**.
- Red is for other disabilities of the body.

"Listening" doesn't always mean using your ears. Not all people speak the same way. Some speak with their hands, in writing, or by using other means.

Diverse Disabilities

Many people have a disability of some sort. Some people have more than one. A disability is a **physical** or **mental** issue that can make it harder to do certain things and interact with the world. It can affect the senses or how people move, learn, or communicate. Sometimes you can tell someone has a disability by looking at them. Sometimes, you can't.

Even if two or more people have the same disability, they're different people. Don't **assume** that everyone in any group is the same, even if you're in that group too! Everyone has different wants and needs. People are **diverse**.

Someone who's blind might have a guide dog to help them get around. Other people might prefer to use a cane.

Learn More

Autism is considered a disability. Being blind is a disability. Having an illness such as diabetes can be a disability. Having legs that don't work like most people's legs is a disability. See how different these things can be?

Good Listening

So, it's important to listen to be a good ally. But how can you be a *good* listener? There are things that good listeners do and—just as important—don't do! Pay attention. Don't half-listen. Show that you're listening though body language like nodding and turning toward the communicator. Try to pay attention to their tone and expression, or the look on their face. Try not to get distracted, or have your thoughts and attention drawn away.

Don't interrupt. However, if you don't understand something, ask questions that show you've been listening. These are skills that are good in most situations!

If you know someone doesn't care for eye contact, don't force it on them! You can talk with them and show you're paying attention in other ways.

Learn More

One thing some people do to show they're listening is to make eye contact. However, this isn't always welcome or comfortable for some people with autism or other issues, whether they're the communicator or listener.

Valid Feelings

When you're listening to someone talk about their disability or an experience they've had because of it, there are other things you might want to keep in mind. This is true even if you have a disability too, and even if you have the same disability!

If someone tells you something (for example, a way someone treated them because of their disability), hurt or bothered them, believe it! Don't try to explain it away. Their feelings are **valid** even if you don't feel the same way or have the same experience. **Acknowledge** their feelings as real and painful.

Learn More

Some people will try to rationalize how other people treat those with disabilities. This means they try to explain the treatment or make excuses for it. But no matter what the reason, the bad feelings it creates are real.

Don’t tell a friend that they shouldn’t be upset because others don’t understand. Just be there for them and listen.

Help Not Always Wanted

It's important not to assume that everyone with a disability is the same. It's also important not to assume that they need *or* want your help. It can be really upsetting for many people with disabilities if someone runs over to butt into something they had under control. For example, it's very rude to push someone in a wheelchair if they haven't asked you to!

Do listen when people tell you they can do something themselves. Don't act like they can't do it. But if someone does ask for help, give it if you can. Ask them the best way to help.

People with disabilities are allowed to have personal space, just like everyone else! Respect for this is important.

Learn More

If someone who is blind asks you to guide them, don't just grab their arm. Offer them your elbow and let them take it.

Be Aware

It's also important to pay attention to the challenges that people with disabilities can face. This can mean learning to notice **accessibility** issues, even when they don't apply to you. If you don't use a wheelchair, you might not think about what a problem even a single step can be for someone else. If you don't deal with daily **fatigue** from a disability, you might not realize why your friend has issues getting around a bigger school building.

When you do learn to pay attention to these things, you can start to ask questions about them. Listen to the answers from people with different disabilities.

Learn More

Pay attention to the language you use about different disabilities. If you're not sure what words someone prefers you use about their disability, ask them politely!

The most important way to learn more about issues that people with disabilities face is to listen to those people! But you can also read books with diverse characters to help you learn more.

Supporting Role

If people with a certain disability tell you that something is a problem (for example, that a popular school club is held in a room that people who use wheelchairs can't get into), believe them. Then, remember that your best place here is in a supporting role, or part, if you don't deal with that disability yourself.

Listen to them and support their voices in asking for change, but don't talk over them or try to take over! Don't assume you know how the problem can be fixed. For one thing, there might be different fixes for different people with different disabilities.

Backing up your friends when they seek change is very important. Sometimes others will listen to a group more than they'd listen to one or two people.

Take Responsibility

Everyone makes mistakes sometimes. It's not as much fun to listen when someone tells you you've made one, but it's very important. If someone tells you that you did something or said something hurtful about their disability, even if you didn't mean to, you need to listen. Don't say you didn't mean it or that they're wrong to be hurt. That's not up to you. This is true even if you have a disability too.

If this happens, listen without interrupting. Then **apologize** and mean it. Take responsibility for what you did or said, and don't do it again.

Learn More

Don't try to pet or play with a service animal while it's working! It has a job to do, and distracting it can harm it or its person.

If someone tells you that you did something wrong, you might want to get mad. But take time to cool down and listen.

Not Just a Disability

When someone has a disability, it can be a big part of their life and their **identity**. Disability pride means that everyone can feel proud of what makes them different and **unique**. Disabilities and differences are not something to be ashamed of or to be hidden.

But it's important to remember that no one is *just* a disability. No one wants to talk about one thing all the time, even if it is a big part of their life. You and your friends with different disabilities can talk about all kinds of things. It's always great to be a good listener, no matter what the subject is!

We're all unique in many different ways!

Glossary

accessible: Able to obtain, use, get into, or understand.

acknowledge: To show that something has been received, noticed, or understood.

ally: A person associated with another for support or a common purpose.

apologize: To express regret to something done or said.

assume: To take something as granted or true.

diverse: Having many different types, forms, or ideas.

fatigue: Being exhausted or very tired.

identity: The qualities, beliefs, etc., that make a particular person or group different from others.

mental: Of or relating to the mind.

neurodiversity: Differences in the way the brain processes information.

physical: Relating to the body instead of the mind.

unique: Special or different from anything else.

valid: Real; having good reason.

For More Information

BOOKS

Maich, Kimberly. *Ableism*. Toronto, Canada: Lorimer, 2023.

McAneney, Caitie. *Different But Equal: Appreciating Diversity*. Buffalo, NY: Powerkids Press, 2019.

Rogers, Amy B. *Learning to Listen*. Buffalo, NY: Rosen Young Adult, 2021.

WEBSITES

The Importance of Listening
thinktv.pbslearningmedia.org/resource/the-importance-of-listening-media-gallery/together-we-can/
Learn more about being a good listener from PBS Learning Media.

Spread the Word: Inclusion
www.spreadtheword.global/
This campaign to end the use of an excluding word about disability has expanded to promote all forms of inclusion.

Publisher's note to educators and parents: Our editors have carefully reviewed these websites to ensure that they are suitable for students. Many websites change frequently, however, and we cannot guarantee that a site's future contents will continue to meet our high standards of quality and educational value. Be advised that students should be closely supervised whenever they access the internet.

Index